"A thoughtful review of the purpose and meaning of business and a fresh way to look at honoring and glorifying God in doing business."
— C. WILLIAM POLLARD
Chairman Emeritus, The ServiceMaster Company

"What a great reminder that your business life can be a critical part of how you serve God and impact lives for eternity!"
— DAVE BROWNE
Former CEO, LensCrafters

"In the often challenging integration of the world of business and a life of faith, Dr. Grudem's book provides helpful, easy-to-understand grounding for business leadership."
— JAMES FELLOWES
Former CEO, Fellowes, Inc.

"Too often Christians feel guilty about self-interest choice, acquisition of private property, and the profit motive. Wayne Grudem makes clear how they are part of God's plan for moral lives. What remarkable insight!"
— STEPHEN HAPPEL, PH.D.
Professor Emeritus of Economics, Arizona State University

"Dr. Grudem clearly shows us how our business activities provide unique opportunities to glorify God. His conclusions are insightful, invaluable, and convicting. I'm putting this on my once-a-year refresher reading list to motivate me to a Colossians 3:23-24 work ethic."
— MIKE SEARCY
Managing Director, Ronald Blue & Co., Phoenix, Arizona

"Effectively refuting the claims to ownership of the sphere of human business activity by corporations, governments, and ideologies, Wayne Grudem succinctly details how business is God's design for His glory and our good."
— DAVID PAYNE
Economist, U.S. Department of Commerce, Washington, D.C.

"This book should be required reading for all pastors who love the business practitioners God has placed in their midst. . . . And all business persons will be blessed and encouraged by reading Wayne Grudem's enlightened application of God's Word to the enterprise of business. The book's content is saturated with God's glorious intentions for those called to serve the Lord in business."
—RICHARD C. CHEWNING, PH.D.
Distinguished Scholar in Residence, John Brown University

A brilliant look at the interconnectedness of economic life with spiritual life, and an essential antidote for those who doubt business as a God-honoring and God-glorifying activity.
—BARRY ASMUS, Ph.D.
Senior Economist, National Center for Policy Analysis

BUSINESS
FOR THE GLORY OF
GOD

*The Bible's Teaching on the
Moral Goodness of Business*

WAYNE GRUDEM

WHEATON, ILLINOIS

Library of Congress Cataloging-in-Publication Data
Grudem, Wayne A.
 Business for the glory of God : the Bible's teaching on the moral
goodness of business / Wayne Grudem.
  p. cm.
 Includes bibliographical references and index.
 ISBN 13: 978-1-58134-517-9
 ISBN 10: 1-58134-517-8 (alk. paper)
 1. Business—Biblical teaching. 2. Business—Religious aspects—
Christianity. I. Title.
BS680.B8G78   2003
261.8'5—dc22   2003021248

Crossway is a publishing ministry of Good News Publishers.

LB		26	25	24	23	22	21	20	19	18
26	25	24	23	22	21	20	19	18	17	16

To my father,
ARDEN E. GRUDEM,
who honored and glorified God in his life in business,

and to my mother,
JEAN C. GRUDEM,
whose generosity, kindness, and faith
have been an example to all who know her

CONTENTS

PREFACE

FOR SEVERAL YEARS I have taught classes and done research on the Bible's teachings about a wide range of economic questions—topics like wealth and poverty, saving and giving, work and leisure, buying and selling, borrowing and lending, employers and employees, and use of the earth's resources for productive purposes. The Bible says much about these topics, and a thorough treatment deserves a much larger book than this, one that I am still in the process of writing.

But while my larger book was still unfinished, Ted Yamamori, past president of Food for the Hungry, persuaded me to read a paper on the way some of these topics apply specifically to business activity. I agreed and read a paper called "How Business in Itself Can Glorify God" at the Conference for Holistic Entrepreneurs, which Dr. Yamamori convened at the Regent University Graduate School of Business, October 3-5, 2002. This book is an expanded version of that paper.[1]

I wish to express thanks to many people who have contributed to my thinking or made suggestions on this manuscript, including Barry Asmus, Jerry Brock, David Browne, Diane Hakala, Stephen Happel, David Payne, Steve Uhlmann, and many former students in class discussions. Special thanks are due to David Kotter, a wise and gracious former student (and adjunct faculty member in economics at Trinity College, Deerfield, Illinois) whose knowledge and experience in economics and business have made numerous contributions to my thinking and have significantly influenced what I have written. Yet I have not taken every suggestion from these helpers and friends, and they should not be blamed for any of my mistakes that remain!

I also wish to express appreciation to the administration and boards of Trinity Evangelical Divinity School (where I taught from 1981 to 2001) and Phoenix Seminary (where I now teach) for each granting me a sabbatical during which I have continued to work on a larger book on Biblical principles and economic values, a book that I hope to be able to complete in the near future. And I wish to thank Sovereign Grace Ministries, a group of churches that has encouraged me and supported me with funds for additional research assistance in this larger research project. That research has provided much of the background for the brief overviews that I provide in this book.

I have dedicated this book to my father, Arden Grudem, whose work in the business world and whose generosity made it possible for me to follow his wise counsel and obtain much more formal education than he was ever able to pursue, and whose business dealings, from what I have heard from others for my whole life, always served to honor and glorify God. I have also dedicated it to my mother, Jean Grudem, whose amazing generosity, kindness, honesty, self-sacrifice, and faith have also glorified God through her whole life, and have provided a model that strongly influenced my idea of what kind of person I would hope to be.

Wayne Grudem
Scottsdale, Arizona
September 19, 2003

INTRODUCTION:

A Neglected Way to Glorify God

IS BUSINESS BASICALLY good or evil?

Words like "profit," "competition," "money," and even "business" carry negative moral connotations for many people today. And some people who work in the business world even labor under a faint cloud of guilt, thinking that their work may be necessary, but that from a moral perspective it is probably "neutral" at best. Very few people instinctively think of business as morally good in itself.

Recent business scandals regarding dishonest and illegal activities by giant companies such as Enron and by formerly revered accounting firms such as Arthur Andersen have made it more likely that people will suspect that there must be something in business that *inherently* tends to wrongdoing. And so the idea of business in itself comes under a dark cloud of suspicion. But is that right?

As for the relationship of business to serving God, when people ask how their lives can "glorify God," they aren't usually told, "Go into business."

When students ask, "How can I serve God with my life?" they don't often hear the answer, "Go into business."

When someone explains to a new acquaintance, "I work

in such-and-such a business," he doesn't usually hear the response, "What a great way to glorify God!"

But that is exactly what this book is going to claim. I am going to argue that many aspects of business activity are morally good *in themselves,* and that *in themselves* they bring glory to God—though they also have great potential for misuse and wrongdoing.

I realize that to most people, the expression "glorifying God" sounds like—well, it just sounds like it belongs *in church,* not in the business world. When people hear the phrase "glorifying God," it probably first implies *worship*—singing praise to God and giving thanks to him. Then it might suggest *evangelism*—glorifying God by telling others about him. It might even suggest *giving*—glorifying God by contributing money to evangelism, to building up the church, and to the needs of the poor. Or it might suggest *moral living*—acting in a way that honors God. Finally, the expression "glorifying God" might suggest a life of *faith*—depending on God in prayer and in our daily attitudes of heart. These five—worship, evangelism, giving, moral living, and faith—are certainly appropriate ways to glorify God. But they are not my focus in this book.

Instead of these things, I want to look at business *in itself*—not just the ways business can contribute to work the church is already doing. In specific, I want to look at the following aspects of business activity:

1. Ownership
2. Productivity
3. Employment

4. Commercial transactions (buying and selling)
5. Profit
6. Money
7. Inequality of possessions
8. Competition
9. Borrowing and lending
10. Attitudes of heart
11. Effect on world poverty

But before considering those things we need to consider two introductory points, the first dealing with the imitation of God, and the second dealing with moral wrongdoing, or sin.

IMITATION: GOD ENJOYS SEEING HIS CHARACTER REFLECTED IN OUR LIVES

One way that we can glorify God is often overlooked. This additional way to glorify God is the key to understanding why God made the world the way he did. It is also the key to understanding why God gave us the moral commands he did. And it is the key to understanding why human beings have an instinctive drive to work, to be productive, to invent, to earn and save and give, and to do the thousands of specific activities that fill our days. This additional way to glorify God is *imitation*—imitation of the attributes of God.

God created us so that we would imitate him and so that he could look at us and see something of his wonderful attributes reflected in us. The first chapter of the Bible tells us,

> So God created man in his own image, in the image of God he created him; male and female he created them (Gen. 1:27).

To be in God's image means to be *like* God and to *represent*
God on the earth. This means that God created us to be more
like him than anything else he made. He delights to look at us and
see in us a reflection of his excellence. After God had created Adam
and Eve,

> God saw everything he had made, and behold, it was *very*
> *good* (Gen. 1:31).[1]

He looked at his creation and took delight in it—yes, in all of
it, but especially in human beings made in his image.

This is why Paul commands us, in Ephesians 5,

> *Be imitators of God,* as beloved children (Eph. 5:1).

If you are a parent, you know that there is a special joy
that comes when you see your children imitating some of your
good qualities and following some of the moral standards that
you have tried to model. When we feel that joy as parents, it is
just a faint echo of what God feels when he sees us, as his children, imitating *his* excellent qualities. "Be imitators of God, as
beloved children."

This idea of imitating God explains many of the com-
mands in the Bible. For instance, "We love *because he first loved*
us" (1 John 4:19). We imitate God's love when we act in love.
Or, "You shall be holy, *for I am holy"* (1 Pet. 1:16, quoting
Lev. 11:44). Similarly, Jesus taught, "Be merciful, *even as your*
Father is merciful" (Luke 6:36). And he also said, "You therefore
must be perfect, *as your heavenly Father is perfect"* (Matt. 5:48).
God wants us to be like him.

This idea of imitating God's character so that he will take delight in us explains other moral commands in the Bible as well. For example, God wants us to tell the truth and not lie because he is the God "who never lies" (Titus 1:2). He commands us not to commit adultery because he is a God who is faithful to his covenant commitments and he delights in seeing us be faithful to the covenant of marriage which we have entered into (see Mal. 2:14). And God commands children to "Honor your father and your mother" (Ex. 20:12; quoted in Eph. 6:2), as a reflection of the honor that the Son gives to the Father in the Trinity.

God created us in such a way that we would *want* to imitate his character. He created us in such a way that we would take spontaneous *delight* in seeing reflections of his character in our own actions and in the actions of others. Though this process is now marred by sin, we still see it happening to some extent. We feel a deep, fulfilling kind of joy and satisfaction in telling the truth (because God is truthful), treating others fairly (because God is fair and just), acting in love toward other people (because God is love), being faithful to our marriages and keeping our word in other commitments (because God is faithful), and so forth. We also enjoy seeing other people act in these ways, because in those actions we catch a glimpse of the character of God. In this way we can begin to understand how to fulfill the command, "So, whether you eat or drink, or whatever you do, do all to the glory of God" (1 Cor. 10:31).

BUT SIN DOES NOT GLORIFY GOD

However, it is absolutely important to realize that we should never attempt to glorify God by acting in ways that disobey his Word. For example, if I were to speak the truth about my neighbor out of a malicious desire to harm him, I would not be glorifying God by imitating his truthfulness, because God's truthfulness is always consistent with all his other attributes, including his attribute of love. And when we read about a thief who robbed a bank through an intricate and skillful plan, we should not praise God for this thief's imitation of divine wisdom and skill, for God's wisdom is always manifested in ways that are consistent with his moral character, which cannot do evil, and consistent with his attributes of love and truthfulness. And thus we must be careful never to try to imitate God's character in ways that contradict his moral law in the Bible.

WHAT THIS BOOK IS NOT

One more thing must be said before we begin. This is not a book on "how to decide the hard ethical questions in business." That would require a longer book than this. In fact, I hope in the future to write on some of the complex ethical questions that confront people every day in the business world.

But before considering the complex challenges in business ethics, it is immensely valuable to understand some of the *fundamental components* of business *in themselves*. Are things like profit, competition, money, and ownership of possessions *always* tainted with evil? Or are they merely *morally neutral* things that can be used for good or for evil? In contrast to those two views, this book will argue that they are all *fundamentally good* things that God has given to the human race, but that they all carry many temptations to misuse and wrongdoing. And even if this book is too short to solve all the complex problems in the "gray areas" of business ethics, there are many things in each aspect of business that are clearly right and wrong, and I will mention those things below as well.

SPECIFIC WAYS THAT BUSINESS CAN GLORIFY GOD

With this background we can now turn to consider specific aspects of business activity, and ask how they provide unique opportunities for glorifying God. We will find that in every aspect of business there are multiple layers of opportunities to give glory to God, as well as multiple temptations to sin.

1

OWNERSHIP

*Owning possessions is fundamentally good and
provides many opportunities for glorifying God,
but also many temptations to sin*

SOMETIMES PEOPLE THINK of all ownership of property as a
kind of "greed" that is morally tainted, and they imagine that
in a perfect world people would not even own personal possessions. But the Bible does not support that idea. When God
gave the command,

"You shall not steal" (Ex. 20:15),

he affirmed the validity of personal ownership of possessions.
I should not steal your car, because it *belongs* to you, not to
me. Unless God intended us to *own* personal possessions, the
command not to steal would make no sense.

I believe the reason God gave the command, "You shall not
steal," is that ownership of possessions is a fundamental way
that we imitate God's sovereignty over the universe by our exer-
cising "sovereignty" over a tiny portion of the universe, the
things we own. When we take care of our possessions, we imi-

tate God in his taking care of the whole universe, and he delights to see us imitate him in this way. In addition, when we care for our possessions, it gives us opportunity to imitate many other attributes of God, such as wisdom, knowledge, beauty, creativity, love for others, kindness, fairness, independence, freedom, exercise of will, blessedness (or joy), and so forth.

Now sometimes Christians refer to ownership as "stewardship," to remind us that what we "own" we do not own absolutely, but only as stewards taking care of what really belongs to God. This is because "the earth is the LORD's and the fullness thereof" (Ps. 24:1) and so ultimately it all belongs to him (see also Lev. 25:23; Ps. 50:10-12; Hag. 2:8; Luke 16:12; 1 Cor. 4:7).

Why do children from a very early age enjoy having toys that are their own, and why do they often want to have a pet that is their own, one they can care for? I realize that such "ownership" of toys and pets can be distorted by the sins of selfishness and laziness, but even if we lived in a sinless world children from a very young age would have a desire to have things that are their own. I think God has created us with *a desire to own things* because he wanted us to have *a desire to imitate his sovereignty* in this way. This desire in itself should not automatically be called "greed," because that word slanders something that is a good desire given to us by God.

When we are responsible stewards, whether taking care of our toys at the age of four or managing the entire factory at the age of forty, if we do this work "as unto the Lord," God looks at our imitation of his sovereignty and his other attributes, and he is pleased. In this way we are his image-bearers, people who are like God and who represent God on the earth, whether we own few possessions or many, and whether we own a small business or a large one.

So what should we do with the things we own? There are many good things to do, all of which can glorify God. One good "use" of our resources—paradoxically—is that we should give some of them away! This is so that *others* can use them wisely, not just we ourselves. For example, we can give to the church to help its evangelism and teaching, and in that way we build up the church. Or we can give some of our possessions to meet the needs of others, especially the poor:

> Do not neglect to do good and to share what you have, for such sacrifices are pleasing to God (Heb. 13:16).

The Bible frequently speaks of the importance of regularly giving away some of what we have been given:

> Honor the LORD with your wealth
>   and with the firstfruits of all your produce (Prov. 3:9).

> . . . we must help the weak and remember the words of the Lord Jesus, how he himself said, "It is more blessed to give than to receive" (Acts 20:35).

Giving is important because it demonstrates trust in God. When I give away $100, I am essentially saying, "God, I am trusting you to provide for $100 of my future needs, because I no longer can depend on this $100." Thus, giving money away shifts our trust from our money to our God. God is pleased when we give ("God loves a cheerful giver," 2 Cor. 9:7) because it not only demonstrates trust in him but also reflects his love for others, his mercy, his compassion for those in need.

But we do not need to give away all that we have! The Bible talks about other morally right uses of our resources as well. For example, a man who owns a tractor can use it *to help "subdue" the earth* (Gen. 1:28)—that is, make the earth useful for us as human beings—by causing the earth to yield corn and beans. People who own more complex equipment can extract materials from the earth to make plastics and silicon in order to make computers and cell phones and Palm Pilots.

At other times, we should use our possessions not to make other goods but simply *for our own enjoyment,* with thanksgiving to God,

> who richly provides us with everything to enjoy
> (1 Tim. 6:17).

It is also right *to save* some of our resources for future use. This will enable us in the future to provide for our relatives, and especially for members of our own households, as God's Word tells us we should do (see 1 Tim. 5:8). We can glorify God through all of these uses of resources if we have thanksgiving in our hearts to God.

On the other hand, ownership of possessions provides many temptations to misuse the resources that God has entrusted to us. We can use our resources to pollute and destroy the earth, or to rob and oppress others, thereby disobeying Jesus' command to love our neighbors as ourselves

(Matt. 22:39), and thereby dishonoring God by our actions. The author of Proverbs 30 knew that stealing is not imitating God but is showing to the world a picture of a God who is self-ish and unjust, for he said,

> . . . lest I be poor and steal
> *and profane the name of my God* (Prov. 30:9).

Or we could use our possessions to turn people away from the gospel and attack the church, as some wealthy people did in the first century:

> Are not the rich the ones who oppress you, and the ones who drag you into court? Are they not the ones who blaspheme the honorable name by which you were called? (James 2:6-7).

We could also use our resources to advance our own pride, or we could become greedy and accumulate wealth for its own sake, or we could take wrongful security in riches (see Matt. 6:19; Luke 12:13-21; James 5:3). We could use our possessions foolishly and wastefully, abounding in luxury and self-indulgence while we neglect the needs of others (see James 5:5; 1 John 3:17). These things are rightly called "material*ism,*" and they are wrong.

In many parts of the world, the wonderful, God-given privilege of owning and managing property is not possible for large segments of the population. In some cultures, property rights are selfishly hoarded by a small number of powerful people and government regulations are so complex and time-consuming that they effectively make it impossible for poor people to own any property or to own a small business.[1] In Communist countries, most private ownership of homes and businesses is prohibited by law, and the government owns all factories and all real estate. Such systems are evil because they prevent people from owning anything more than a small number of personal possessions, and thus they prevent people from even having the opportunity to glorify God through owning any property, or owning a home or a business.

Ownership can be abused, but the distortions of something good must not cause us to think that the thing itself is evil. Possessions are not evil in themselves, and the ownership of possessions is not wrong in itself. Nor is ownership something morally neutral. In itself, the ownership of possessions is something that is created by God, and very good. Ownership provides multiple opportunities for glorifying God, and we should be thankful for it.

2

PRODUCTIVITY

*Producing goods and services is fundamentally good
and provides many opportunities for glorifying God,
but also many temptations to sin*

WE KNOW THAT producing goods from the earth is fundamentally good in itself because it is part of the purpose for which God put us on the earth. Before there was sin in the world, God put Adam in the garden of Eden "to work it and keep it" (Gen. 2:15), and God told both Adam and Eve, before there was sin,

> "Be fruitful and multiply and fill the earth and *subdue it* and *have dominion* over the fish of the sea and over the birds of the heavens and over every living thing that moves on the earth" (Gen. 1:28).

The word translated "subdue" (Hebrew *kābash*) implies that Adam and Eve should make the resources of the earth useful for their own benefit, and this implies that God intended them to develop the earth so that they could come to own agricultural products and animals, then housing and works of craftsmanship and beauty, and eventually buildings, means of transportation, cities, and inventions of all sorts.

Manufactured products give us opportunity to praise God for anything we look at in the world around us. Imagine what would happen if we were able somehow to transport Adam and Eve, before they had sinned, into a twenty-first-century American home. After we gave them appropriate clothing, we would turn on the faucet to offer them a glass of water, and they would ask, "What's that?" When we explained that the pipes enabled us to have water whenever we wanted it, they would exclaim, "Do you mean to say that God has put in the earth materials that would enable you to make that water system?"

"Yes," we would reply.

"Then *praise God* for giving us such a great earth! And praise him for giving us the knowledge and skill to be able to make that water system!" They would have hearts sensitive to God's desire that he be honored in all things.

The refrigerator would elicit even more praise to God from their lips. And so would the electric lights and the newspaper and the oven and the telephone, and so forth. Their hearts would brim over with thankfulness to the Creator who had hidden such wonderful materials in the earth and had also given to human beings such skill in working with them. And as Adam and Eve's hearts were filled with overflowing thanksgiving to God, God would see it and be pleased. He would look with delight as the man and woman made in his image gave glory to their Creator and fulfilled the purpose for which they were made.

As we look at any manufactured item, no matter how common, can we not also discover hundreds of wonders of God's creation in the things that we have been able to make from the earth? Such richness and variety has not been found on any of the other planets known to us.

> . . . the whole earth is full of his glory (Isa. 6:3).

God did not have to create us with a need for material things or a need for the services of other people (think of the angels, who apparently do not have such needs), but in his wisdom he chose to do so. It may be that God created us with such needs because he knew that *in the process of productive work* we would have many opportunities to glorify him. When we work to produce (for example) pairs of shoes from the earth's resources, God sees us imitating his attributes of wisdom, knowledge, skill, strength, creativity, appreciation of beauty, sovereignty, planning for the future, and the use of language to communicate. In addition, when we produce pairs of shoes to be used by others, we demonstrate love for others, wisdom in understanding their needs, and interdependence and interpersonal cooperation (which are reflections of God's Trinitarian existence). If we do this, as Paul says, while working heartily, "as for the Lord and not for men" (Col. 3:23), and if our hearts have joy and thanksgiving to God as we make this pair of shoes, then God delights to see his excellent character reflected in our lives, and others will see something of God's character in us as well. And so it is with any manufactured good, and any service we perform for wages for the benefit of others. As Jesus said, our light will "shine before others, so that they may see your good works and give glory to your Father who is in heaven" (Matt. 5:16).

That is why God made us with a desire to be productive, to make or do something useful for other people. Therefore human desires to increase the production of goods and services are not in themselves greedy or materialistic or evil. Rather, such desires to be more productive represent God-given desires to accomplish and achieve and solve problems. They represent God-given desires to exercise dominion over the earth and exercise faithful stewardship so that we and others may enjoy the resources of the earth that God made for our use and for our enjoyment.

This is consistent with God's command to Adam and Eve in Genesis 1:28:

> And God said to them, "Be fruitful and multiply and fill the earth and subdue it and have dominion over the fish of the sea and over the birds of the heavens and over every living thing that moves on the earth."

God's command to "subdue" the earth implies doing productive work to make the resources of the earth useful for themselves and others. That is what he wanted Adam and Eve to do, and that is one of the things he wants us to do as well.

Therefore, in contrast to some people's attitude toward life today, *productive work* is not evil or undesirable in itself, or something to be avoided. Productive work should not be seen as "bad," but as something "good." In fact, the Bible does not view positively the idea of retiring early and not working at anything again. Rather, work in itself is also something that is *fundamentally good* and God-given, for it was something that God commanded Adam and Eve to do before there was sin in the world. Although work since the Fall has aspects of pain and futility (see Gen. 3:17-19), it is still not morally neutral but *fundamentally good* and pleasing to God.

Hindering and decreasing the earth's productivity (as when wars destroy factories and farms, or when governments prevent them from operating) is not good, however, because it simply allows the curse that God imposed in Genesis 3 to gain more and more influence in the world, and this is what Satan's goal is, not God's. After God imposed the curse that was required by his justice, the story of the Bible is one of God working progressively to overcome the curse, and increasing the world's productivity is something we should do as one aspect of that task.

But significant temptations accompany all productions of goods and services. There is the temptation for our hearts to be turned from God so that we focus on material things for their own sake. There are also temptations to pride, and to turning our hearts away from love for our neighbor and toward selfishness, greed, and hard-heartedness. There are temptations to produce goods that bring monetary reward but that are harmful and destructive and evil (such as pornography and addictive drugs).

But the distortions of something good must not cause us to think that the thing itself is evil. Increasing the production of goods and services is not morally neutral but is *fundamentally good* and pleasing to God.

3

EMPLOYMENT

Hiring people to do work is fundamentally good and
provides many opportunities for glorifying God,
but also many temptations to sin

IN CONTRAST TO Marxist theory, the Bible does not view it
as evil for one person to hire another person and gain profit
from that person's work. It is not necessarily "exploiting" the
employee. Rather, Jesus said,

> "the laborer deserves his wages" (Luke 10:7),

and by this statement he implicitly approved of the idea of paying wages to employees. In fact, Jesus' parables often speak of
servants and masters, and of people paying others for their
work, with no hint that hiring people to work for wages is evil
or wrong. And John the Baptist told soldiers, "Be content with
your wages" (Luke 3:14).

For some occupations, being employed by someone else is
necessary, because some people sell services and not goods. In
the ancient world, a maid or a messenger or the laborer in a
field would work for someone else; and in the modern world a

teacher or a baby-sitter, or a painter or a plumber, earns money
when hired by another person. But the hiring of one person by
another is also necessary for a greater production of goods.
Many products can only be produced by a group of people
working together. In the ancient world, shipbuilding and ship-
ping could only be done by hiring many people, and in the
modern world, building airplanes, ships, steel mills, and in most
cases houses and computers, and many other consumer goods,
can only be done by hiring other people, because the tasks are
too large and too complicated for one person alone. But working in groups requires the oversight of a manager, and this is
most often an owner who pays the others for their work.

This is a wonderful ability that God has given us. Paying
another person for his or her labor is an activity that is uniquely
human. It is shared by no other creature. The ability to work
for other people for pay, or to pay other people for their work,
is another way that God has created us so that we would be able
to glorify him more fully in such relationships.

Employer/employee relationships provide many opportunities for glorifying God. On both sides of the transaction, we
can imitate God, and he will take pleasure in us when he sees
us showing honesty, fairness, trustworthiness, kindness, wisdom and skill, and keeping our word regarding how much we
promised to pay or what work we agreed to do. The employer/
employee relationship also gives opportunity to demonstrate
proper exercise of authority and proper responses to authority,
in imitation of the authority that has eternally existed between
the Father and Son in the Trinity.

When the employer/employee arrangement is working

properly, both parties benefit. This allows love for the other person to manifest itself. For example, let's say that I have a job sewing shirts in someone else's shop. I can honestly seek the good of my employer, and seek to sew as many shirts as possible for him along with attention to quality (compare 1 Tim. 6:2), and he can seek my good, because he will pay me at the end of the week for a job well done. As in every good business transaction, both parties end up better off then they were before. In this case, I have more money at the end of the week than I did before, and my employer has more shirts ready to take to market than he did before. And so we have worked together to produce something that did not exist in the world before that week—the world is 500 shirts "wealthier" than it was when the week began. Together we have created some new "wealth" in the world. This is a small example of obeying God's command to "subdue" the earth (Gen. 1:28) and make its resources useful for mankind. Now if we multiply that by millions of plants, millions of workers, and millions of different products, it is evident how the world gains material "wealth" that did not exist before—new products have been created by an employer hiring an employee to manufacture something.

Therefore if you hire me to work in your business, you are doing good for me and you are providing both of us with many opportunities to glorify God. It is the same way with hiring people to produce services—whether hiring teachers to teach in a school, doctors to care for people in a clinic, mechanics to fix cars, or painters to paint houses. The employer/employee relationship enables people to create services for others that were not there before.

However, employer/employee relationships carry many temptations to sin. An employer can exercise his authority with harshness and oppression and unfairness. He might withhold pay arbitrarily and unreasonably (contrary to Lev. 19:13) or might underpay his workers, keeping wages so low that workers have no opportunity to improve their standard of living (contrary to Deut. 24:14). He might also become puffed-up with pride. James writes about such sins of oppressive employers:

> Behold, the wages of the laborers who mowed your fields, which you kept back by fraud, are crying out against you, and the cries of the harvesters have reached the ears of the Lord of hosts (James 5:4).

Employees also have temptations to sin through carelessness in work (see Prov. 18:9), laziness, jealousy, bitterness, rebelliousness, dishonesty, or theft (see Titus 2:9-10).

But the distortions of something good must not cause us to think that the thing itself is evil. Employer/employee relationships, in themselves, are not morally neutral but are fundamentally good and pleasing to God because they provide many opportunities to imitate God's character and so glorify him.

4

COMMERCIAL TRANSACTIONS

*Buying and selling are fundamentally good and
provide many opportunities for glorifying God,
but also many temptations to sin*

SEVERAL PASSAGES OF Scripture assume that buying and selling are morally right. Regarding the sale of land in ancient Israel, God's law said,

> "If you make a sale to your neighbor or buy from your neighbor, you shall not wrong one another" (Lev. 25:14).

This implies that it is *possible* and in fact is *expected* that people should buy and sell *without* wronging one another—that is, that both buyer and seller can *do right* in the transaction (see also Gen. 41:57; Lev. 19:35-36; Deut. 25:13-16; Prov. 11:26; 31:16; Jer. 32:25, 42-44).

In fact, buying and selling are necessary for anything beyond subsistence level living, and these activities are another part of what distinguishes us from the animal kingdom. No

individual or family providing for all its own needs could produce more than a very low standard of living (that is, if it could
buy and sell *absolutely nothing,* and had to live off only what it
could produce itself, which would be a fairly simple range of
foods and clothing). But when we can sell what we make and
buy from others who specialize in producing milk or bread,
orange juice or blueberries, bicycles or televisions, cars or computers, then, through the mechanism of buying and selling,
we can all obtain a much higher standard of living, and thereby
fulfill God's purpose that we enjoy the resources of the earth
with thanksgiving (1 Tim. 4:3-5; 6:17) while we "eat" and
"drink" and "do all to the glory of God" (1 Cor. 10:31).

Therefore we should not look at commercial transactions as
a necessary evil or something just morally neutral. Rather, commercial transactions are *in themselves good* because through them
we do good to other people. This is because of the amazing truth
that, in most cases, *voluntary commercial transactions benefit both
parties.* If I sell you a copy of my book for $12, then I get some-
thing that I want more than that copy of the book: I get your
$12. So I am better off than I was before, when I had too many
copies of that book, copies that I was never going to read. And
I am happy. But you got something that you wanted more than
your $12. You wanted a copy of my book, which you did not
have. So you are better off than you were before, and you are
happy. Thus by giving us the ability to buy and sell, God has
given us a wonderful mechanism through which we can do
good for each other. We should be thankful for this process
every time we buy or sell something. We can honestly see buying and selling as one means of loving our neighbor as ourself.

Buying and selling are activities unique to human beings out of all the creatures that God made. Rabbits and squirrels, dogs and cats, elephants and giraffes know nothing of this activity. Through buying and selling God has given us a wonderful means to bring glory to him.

We can imitate God's attributes each time we buy and sell, if we practice honesty, faithfulness to our commitments, fairness, and freedom of choice. Moreover, commercial transactions provide many opportunities for personal interaction, as when I realize that I am buying not just from a store but from a person, to whom I should show kindness and God's grace. In fact, every business transaction is an opportunity for us to be fair and truthful and thus to obey Jesus' teaching,

> "So whatever you wish that others would do to you, do also to them, for this is the Law and the Prophets" (Matt. 7:12).

Because of the interpersonal nature of commercial transactions, business activity has significant stabilizing influence on a society. An individual farmer may not really like the auto mechanic in town very much, and the auto mechanic may not like the farmer very much, but the farmer *does* want his car to be fixed right the next time it breaks down, and the auto mechanic *does* love the sweet corn and tomatoes that the farmer sells; so it is to their mutual advantage to get along with each other, and their animosity is restrained. In fact, they may even seek the good of the other person for this reason! So it is with commercial transactions throughout the world and even between nations. This is an evidence of God's common grace, because in the mechanism of buying and selling God has provided the human race with a wonderful encouragement to love our neighbor by pursuing actions that advance not only our own welfare but also the welfare of others—even as we pursue our own. In buying and selling we also manifest interdependence and thus reflect the interdependence and interpersonal love among the members of the Trinity. Therefore, for those who have eyes to see it, commercial transactions provide another means of manifesting the glory of God in our lives.

However, commercial transactions provide many temptations to sin. Rather than seeking the good of our neighbors as well as ourselves, our hearts can be filled with greed, so that we seek only our own good, and give no thought for the good of others. (This would happen, for example, when one person in a business transaction wants 99 percent or 100 percent of the benefit and wants the other person to be reduced to 1 percent or 0 percent of the benefit.) Or our hearts can be overcome with selfishness, an inordinate desire for wealth, and setting our hearts only on material gain. Paul says,

> Those who desire to be rich fall into temptation, into a snare, into many senseless and harmful desires that plunge people into ruin and destruction. For the love of money is a root of all kinds of evils. It is through this craving that some have wandered away from the faith and pierced themselves with many pangs (1 Tim. 6:9-10).

Because of sin, we can also engage in dishonesty and in selling shoddy materials whose defects are covered with glossy paint. Where there is excessive concentration of power or a huge imbalance in knowledge, there will often be oppression of those who lack power or knowledge (as in government-sponsored monopolies where consumers are only allowed access to poor quality, high-priced goods from one manufacturer for each product).

Sadly, even some who call themselves Christians are dishonest in their business dealings. I have heard several stories from Christian friends about how other so-called "Christians" have broken their word, "forgotten" their business promises or failed to keep them, betrayed a partner's trust, done shoddy work, or been dishonest about a product or the condition of a company. These actions by a small minority in the Christian community bring reproach on the whole church and bring dishonor to the name of Jesus Christ. Such actions should not be swept under the rug, but should be subject to the process of personal confrontation and church discipline that Jesus outlines in Matthew 18:15-20.

But the distortions of something good must not cause us to think that the thing itself is evil. Commercial transactions in themselves are fundamentally right and pleasing to God. They are a wonderful gift from him through which he has enabled us to have many opportunities to glorify him.

5

PROFIT

*Earning a profit is fundamentally good and
provides many opportunities for glorifying God,
but also many temptations to sin*

WHAT IS EARNING A PROFIT? Fundamentally, it is selling a product for more than the cost of producing it. If I have a bakery and bake 100 loaves of bread at a cost of $100, but sell them for a total of $200, I have made $100 profit. But if people are willing to pay $2 for each of my loaves of bread, it means that they think what I have produced is valuable—the bread that cost me $1 is worth $2 to them! This shows that my work has added *some value* to the materials I used. Profit is thus an indication that I have made something useful for others, and in that way it can show that I am doing good for others in the goods and services that I sell.

In addition, profit can indicate that I have used resources more efficiently than others, because when my costs are lower, my profit is higher. If another baker wasted some flour and some yeast and spent $125 to make 100 loaves, then his profit was less than mine. But using resources more efficiently (not wasting them) is also something good, since there are more and cheaper resources that remain for others to use as well. Therefore profit is an indication that I am making good and efficient use of the earth's resources, thus obeying God's original "creation mandate" to "subdue" the earth:

> "Be fruitful and multiply and fill the earth and *subdue it* and have dominion over the fish of the sea and over the birds of the heavens and over every living thing that moves on the earth" (Gen. 1:28).

In the parable of the minas (or pounds), Jesus tells of a nobleman calling ten of his servants and giving them one mina each (about three months' wages), and telling them, "Engage in business until I come" (Luke 19:13). The servant who earned 1,000 percent profit was rewarded greatly, for when he says, "Lord, your mina has made ten minas more," the nobleman responds,

> "Well done, good servant! Because you have been faithful in a very little, you shall have authority over ten cities" (v. 17).

The servant who made five more minas receives authority over five cities, and *the one who made no profit is rebuked* for not at least putting the mina in the bank to earn interest (v. 23).

The nobleman of course represents Jesus himself, who went to a far country to receive a kingdom and then returned to reward his servants. The parable has obvious applications to stewardship of spiritual gifts and ministries that Jesus entrusts to us, but in order for the parable to make sense, it has to assume that *good stewardship, in God's eyes, includes expanding and multiplying whatever resources or stewardship God has entrusted to you.* Surely we cannot exclude money and material possessions from the application of the parable, for they are part of what God entrusts to each of us, and our money and possessions can and should be used to glorify God. Seeking profit, therefore, or seeking to multiply our resources, is seen as fundamentally good. Not to do so is condemned by the master when he returns.

The parable of the talents (Matt. 25:14-30) has a similar point, but the amounts are larger, for a talent was worth about twenty years' wages for a laborer, and different amounts are given at the outset.

A similar assumption is behind the approval given to the ideal wife in Proverbs 31:

She perceives that her merchandise is profitable (v. 18).

The word translated "merchandise" (Hebrew *śachar*) refers to profit-producing commercial transactions. This "excellent wife" is commended for selling goods for a profit.

Some people will object that earning a profit is "exploiting" other people. Why should I charge you $2 for a loaf of bread if it only cost me $1 to produce? One reason is that you are paying not only for my raw materials but also for my work as an "entrepreneur"—my time in baking the bread, my baking skill that I learned at the cost of more of my time, my skill in finding and organizing the materials and equipment to bake bread, and (significantly) for the risks I take in baking 100 loaves of bread each day before any buyers have even entered my shop!

In any society, some people are too cautious by nature to

assume the risks involved in starting and running a business, but others are willing to take that risk, and it is right to give them some *profit* as a reward for taking those risks that benefit all the rest of us. It is the hope of such reward that motivates people to start businesses and assume such risks. If profit were not allowed in a society, then people would not take such risks, and we would have very few goods available to buy. Allowing profit, therefore, is a very good thing that brings benefits to everybody in the society.

Of course, there can be wrongful profit. For example, if there is a great disparity in power or knowledge between you and me and I take advantage of that and cheat you, I would not be obeying Jesus' command,

> "So whatever you wish that others would do to you, do also to them, for this is the Law and the Prophets" (Matt. 7:12).

Or if I am in charge of a monopoly on a necessary good, so that people can only buy bread or water or gasoline from me and no other suppliers can enter the market, and if I then charge an exorbitant price that depletes people's wealth, of course that kind of profit is excessive and wrong. That is where earning a profit provides temptations to sin.

But the distortions of something good must not cause us to think that the thing itself is evil. If profit is made in a system of voluntary exchange not distorted by monopoly power or dishonesty or greatly unequal knowledge, then when I earn a profit I also help you. You are better off because you have a loaf of bread that you wanted, and I am better off because I earned $1 profit, and that keeps me in business and makes me want to make more bread to sell. Everybody wins, and nobody is exploited. Through this process, as my business profits and grows, I continue to glorify God by enlarging the possessions over which I am "sovereign" and over which I can exercise wise stewardship.

The ability to earn a profit thus results in multiplying our resources while helping other people. It is a wonderful ability that God gave us and it is not evil or morally neutral, but is fundamentally good. Through it we can reflect many of God's attributes, such as love for others, wisdom, sovereignty, and planning for the future.

6

MONEY

*Money is fundamentally good and provides many
opportunities for glorifying God, but also
many temptations to sin*

PEOPLE SOMETIMES SAY that "money is the root of all evil," but
the Bible does not say that. Paul says in 1 Timothy 6:10,

the *love of money* is a root of all kinds of evils,

but that speaks of the love of money, not money itself.

In fact, *money is fundamentally good* because it is a human
invention that sets us apart from the animal kingdom and
enables us to subdue the earth by producing from the earth
goods and services that bring benefit to others. Money enables
all of mankind to be productive and enjoy the fruits of that
productivity thousands of times more extensively than we
could if no human being had money, and we just had to barter
with each other.

Without money, I would have only one thing to trade
with, and that is copies of my books. I would have hundreds
of copies of my book *Systematic Theology,*[1] for example, but in

a world with no money I would have no idea if one volume was worth a loaf of bread, or two shirts, or a bicycle, or a car. And the grocer might not be interested in reading my book, so he might not trade me a basket of groceries for even 100 books! Soon even the merchants who did accept my book in trade would not want another one, or a third one, and I would end up with piles of books and no ability to find more people who wanted to trade something for them. Without money, I would soon be forced to revert to subsistence living by planting a garden and raising cows and chickens, and maybe bartering a few eggs from time to time. And so would you, with whatever you could produce.

But money is the one thing that *everybody* is willing to trade goods for, because it is the one thing that *everybody else* is willing to trade goods for. With a system of money, I suddenly know how much one volume of my book is worth. It is worth $40, because that is how much thousands of people have decided they are willing to pay for it.

Money also stores the value of something until I spend it on something else. When I get the $40, that money temporarily holds the value of my book until I can go to the store and tell the grocer I would like to trade the $40 for some groceries. The same grocer who would not have traded *any* groceries for a theology book now eagerly accepts my $40 in money, because he knows that he can trade that money for *anything in the world* that he wants and that costs $40.

So money is simply a tool for our use, and we can rightly thank God that in his wisdom he ordained that we would invent it and use it. It is simply a "medium of exchange," something that makes voluntary exchanges possible. It is

> a commodity . . . that is legally established as an exchangeable equivalent of all other commodities, such as goods and services, and is used as a measure of their comparative values on the market.[2]

Money makes voluntary exchanges more fair, less wasteful, and far more extensive. We need money in the world in order for us to be good stewards of the earth and to glorify God through using it wisely.

If money were evil in itself, then God would not have any. But he says,

> "The silver is mine, and the gold is mine, declares the LORD of hosts" (Hag. 2:8).

It all belongs to him, and he entrusts it to us so that through it we would glorify him.

Money provides many opportunities to glorify God: through investing and expanding our stewardship and thus imitating God's sovereignty and wisdom; through meeting our own needs and thus imitating God's independence; through giving to others and thus imitating God's mercy and love; or through giving to the church and to evangelism and thus bringing others into the kingdom.

Yet because money carries so much power and so much value, it is a heavy responsibility, and it presents constant temptations to sin. We can become ensnared in the love of money

(1 Tim. 6:10), and it can turn our hearts from God. Jesus warned, "You cannot serve God and money" (Matt. 6:24), and he warned against accumulating too much that we hoard and do not use for good:

> "Do not lay up for yourselves treasures on earth, where moth and rust destroy and where thieves break in and steal, but lay up for yourselves treasures in heaven, where neither moth nor rust destroys and where thieves do not break in and steal. For where your treasure is, there your heart will be also" (Matt. 6:19-21).

But the distortions of something good must not cause us to think that the thing itself is evil. Money is good in itself, and provides us many opportunities for glorifying God.

INEQUALITY OF POSSESSIONS

*Some inequality of possessions is fundamentally good
and provides many opportunities for glorifying God,
but also many temptations to sin; and some
extreme inequalities are wrong in themselves*

IT MAY SEEM SURPRISING to us to think that some inequalities of possessions can be good and pleasing to God. However, although there is no sin or evil in heaven, the Bible teaches that there are varying degrees of reward in heaven and various kinds of stewardship that God entrusts to different people. When we stand before Jesus to give account of our lives, he will say to one person,

"You shall have authority over ten cities,"

and to another,

"You are to be over five cities" (Luke 19:17, 19).

Therefore there will be inequalities of stewardship and responsibility in the age to come. This means that the idea of inequality of stewardship in itself is given by God and must be good.

In a similar teaching, Paul, speaking to believers, says, "For *we must all appear before the judgment seat of Christ,* so that each one may receive *what is due for what he has done in the body,* whether good or evil" (2 Cor. 5:10). This implies *degrees of reward* for what we have done in this life. Many other passages teach or imply degrees of reward for believers at the final judgment.[1] Even among the angels, there are differing levels of authority and stewardship established by God, and therefore we cannot say that such a system is wrong or sinful in itself.

Inequalities are necessary in a world that requires a great variety of tasks to be done. Some tasks require stewardship of large amounts of resources (such as ownership of a steel mill or a company that manufactures airplanes), and some tasks require stewardship of small amounts of resources. And God has given some people greater abilities than others, abilities in artistic or musical skills, abilities in mathematics or science, abilities in leadership, abilities in business skills and buying and selling, and so forth. If reward for each person's labor is given fairly and is based on the value of what that person produces, then those with larger abilities will naturally gain larger rewards. Since people are different in abilities and effort, I don't think there could be a fair system of rewards for work unless the system had different rewards for different people. Fairness of reward requires such differences.

In fact, God has never had a goal of producing equality of possessions among people, and he will never do so. In the Year of Jubilee (Leviticus 25), agricultural land returned to its previous owner and debts were canceled, but there was no equalizing of money or jewels or cattle or sheep, and houses inside walled cities did not revert to the previous owner (v. 30).

Some people have seen an argument for equal possessions in 2 Corinthians 8, but there Paul did not say that God's goal was equality. For example, he did not tell the wealthy Corinthians to send money to the poor Macedonians mentioned in 2 Corinthians 8:1-5, but only that they should contribute their fair share in helping the famine-stricken Christians in Jerusalem:

> . . . as a matter of *fairness* your abundance at the present time should supply their need, so that their abundance may supply your need, that there may be *fairness* (2 Cor. 8:13-14, ESV; the Greek word *isotēs* also means "fairness" in Col. 4:1, where it cannot mean "equality").

Nor does the book of Acts teach some kind of "early communism" when it says that believers had all things in common. It is important to look at the passages carefully:

> And all who believed were together and had all things in common. And they were selling their possessions and belongings and distributing the proceeds to all, as any had need. And day by day, attending the temple together and breaking bread in their homes, they received their food with glad and generous hearts . . . (Acts 2:44-46).

> Now the full number of those who believed were of one heart and soul, and no one said that any of the things that belonged to him was his own, but they had everything in common. And with great power the apostles were giving

their testimony to the resurrection of the Lord Jesus, and
great grace was upon them all. There was not a needy person among them, for as many as were owners of lands or
houses sold them and brought the proceeds of what was sold
and laid it at the apostles' feet, and it was distributed to
each as any had need (Acts 4:32-35).

These texts certainly show an amazing level of trust in God,
generosity, and love for one another, all as a result of a remarkable
outpouring of the Holy Spirit's power in a time of great revival.
But it is a great mistake to call this "early communism," for
(1) the giving was voluntary and was not compelled by the government, and (2) people still had personal possessions, because
they still met in "their homes" (Acts 2:46), and many other
Christians later still owned homes, such as Mary, the mother of
John Mark (Acts 12:12), Jason (Acts 17:5), Titius Justus (Acts
18:7), many Christians in Ephesus (Acts 20:20), Philip the evan-
gelist (Acts 21:8), Mnason of Cyprus (Acts 21:16, in Jerusalem),
Priscilla and Aquila in Rome (Rom. 16:5; 1 Cor. 16:19),
Nympha (Col. 4:15), Philemon (Philem. 2), and other
Christians in general to whom John wrote (2 John 10).

Immediately after the description of such amazing generosity in Acts 4, there is in chapter 5 the story of Ananias and
Sapphira, who lied about the sale price of some land. But Peter
tells them there was no need to do this:

> "While it remained unsold, did it not remain your own?
> And after it was sold, was it not at your disposal? Why is it
> that you have contrived this deed in your heart? You have
> not lied to men but to God" (Acts 5:4).

It is significant that this story occurs immediately after the paragraph that says "they had everything in common" (Acts 4:32). It reminds us that all of that generosity in Acts 4 was voluntary and was not intended to nullify the ideas of individual ownership or inequality of possessions. When Peter says,

> "While it remained unsold, did it not remain your own?
> And after it was sold, was it not at your disposal?"

he reaffirms the idea of private property and keeps us from the mistaken idea that the church was establishing a new requirement that Christians give up all private property, or that Christians all had to have equal possessions. Acts 5:4 guards against such misunderstandings.

Later in the New Testament, when Paul gives specific instructions to those who are wealthy, he does not tell them to give up all their possessions, but to be generous and to set their hearts on God, not on their wealth:

> As for the rich in this present age, charge them not to be haughty, nor to set their hopes on the uncertainty of riches, but on God, who richly provides us with everything to enjoy. They are to do good, to be rich in good works, to be generous and ready to share, thus storing up treasure for themselves as a good foundation for the future, so that they may take hold of that which is truly life (1 Tim. 6:17-19).

So we should not think of all inequalities of possessions as wrong, or as evil. In fact, inequalities in possessions provide many opportunities for glorifying God.

If God gives us a small stewardship with regard to material possessions or abilities and opportunities, then we can glorify him through being content in him, trusting in him for our needs, expecting reward from him, and being faithful to our commitments. In fact, those who are poor often give more sacrificially than those who are rich. Jesus saw a poor widow put a penny in the offering, and he told his disciples,

> "Truly, I say to you, this poor widow has put in more than all those who are contributing to the offering box. For they all contributed out of their abundance, but she out of her poverty has put in everything she had, all she had to live on" (Mark 12:43-44).

And James tells us,

> Has not God chosen those who are poor in the world to be rich in faith and heirs of the kingdom which he has promised to those who love him? (James 2:5).

Thus, the Bible does not teach a "health and wealth gospel" (at least not until heaven!). In this present age, there are inequalities of gifts and abilities, and there are also evil, oppressive systems in the world, and because of these things many of God's most righteous people will not be rich in this life.

As for those who have large resources, they also are to be content in God and trust in him, not in their riches, and both James and Paul suggest that they face greater temptations (see 1 Tim. 6:9-10; James 2:6-7; 5:1-6). Those who are rich have more opportunities and also more obligation to give generously to the poor (1 Tim. 6:17-19) and to the work of the church (Luke 12:48; 1 Cor. 4:2; 14:12b).

Inequalities in possessions, opportunities, and abilities provide many temptations to sin. There are temptations on the part of the wealthy or those who have other kinds of large stewardships to be proud, to be selfish, to think too highly of themselves, and not to trust in God. On the other hand, those to whom God has entrusted less have temptations to coveting and jealousy and not valuing their own personal position and calling in life, to which God has called them, at least for the present time.

In addition to this, there are some extreme kinds of inequalities in possessions and opportunities that are wrong in themselves. Poverty will not exist in the age to come, and so Jesus' statement, "the poor you always have with you" (John 12:8) is best understood to mean "always in this age." It does not mean that poverty will last forever, even into eternity. Poverty is one of the results of living in a world affected by sin and the Fall, and by God's curse on the productivity of the earth after Adam and Eve sinned (Gen. 3:17-19).

We should seek to help the poor and seek to overcome their poverty. John says,

> If anyone has the world's goods and sees his brother in need, yet closes his heart against him, how does God's love abide in him? (1 John 3:17).

And when Paul went to Jerusalem to confirm the validity of his teaching in conversation with the apostles there, he found that they were in agreement, and then added,

they asked us to remember the poor, the very thing I
was eager to do (Gal. 2:10; see also Matt. 25:39-40; Acts
2:45; 4:35; Rom. 12:13; 15:25-27; Eph. 4:28; Titus
3:14; Heb. 13:16).

The emphasis in the New Testament is on helping *poor
Christians,* especially those who are near us or who come to
our attention (see 1 John 3:17; Matt. 25:39-40; Rom. 15:25-
27; 2 Corinthians 8–9). But it is also right to help non-
Christians who are poor and needy, as we see in the parable of
the Good Samaritan who helped someone in need from a different religious background (Luke 10:25-37). We also see it in
Jesus' teaching, where he told us,

> "love your enemies, and do good and lend, expecting noth-
> ing in return, and your reward will be great, and you will
> be sons of the Most High; for he is kind to the ungrateful
> and the evil" (Luke 6:35; compare also Jesus' practice of
> healing all who came to him, not just those who believed
> in him as the Messiah).

So the New Testament emphasis on helping the poor shows
us that there is an extreme kind of inequality that is not good,
a point where people are in poverty and should be helped.
(Just what "poverty" is will vary from society to society and
will also vary over time within any one society.)

But is there an opposite extreme of having too much
wealth? In contrast to many admonitions to help the poor,
there is no corresponding command in the New Testament to
take some wealth away from the very rich, and there is no

teaching that a large amount of wealth is wrong in itself. But there are strong warnings against spending too much on one-self and living in self-indulgent luxury:

> Come now, you rich, weep and howl for the miseries that are coming upon you. . . . Your gold and silver have cor-roded, and their corrosion will be evidence against you and will eat your flesh like fire. You have laid up treasure in the last days. . . . You have lived on the earth in luxury and in self-indulgence. You have fattened your hearts in a day of slaughter (James 5:1, 3, 5).

James does not here imply that *all* those who are rich are evil, for in this same passage he speaks of the fraud and mur-der committed by these rich people, implying that he is speak-ing about the rich who are wrongdoers (James 5:4, 6). Paul says that Timothy should tell "the rich in this present age" that they are "not to be haughty, nor to set their hopes on the uncer-tainty of riches, but on God, who richly provides us with every-thing to enjoy." Paul does not say that the rich are to give away all their wealth, but that they are "to do good, to be rich in good works, to be generous and ready to share" (1 Tim. 6:17-18).

Yet James clearly warns against a kind of "luxury and self-indulgence" that is wrong, that shows little or no concern for others, and that does not take seriously the stewardship obli-gations that God bestows along with great wealth. It seems that those who are wealthy can too easily slip beyond a level of spending on themselves that is appropriate to their place in life and spend excessively and ostentatiously on themselves while neglecting to give generously to others.

But the distortions of something good must not cause us to think that the thing itself is evil. The evils of poverty and excessive, self-indulgent wealth must not cause us to think that God's goal is total equality of possessions, or that all inequalities are wrong. Inequalities in abilities and opportunities and possessions will be part of our life in heaven forever, and they are in themselves good and pleasing to God, and provide many opportunities for glorifying him.

8

COMPETITION

*Competition is fundamentally good and provides
many opportunities for glorifying God,
but also many temptations to sin*

AS WITH OTHER ASPECTS of business that we have considered, so it is with competition: the evils and distortions that have sometimes accompanied competition have led people to the conclusion that competition is evil in itself. But this is not true.

We can think of some good examples of competition in other areas of life. To take one example, most people think competition in sports is a good thing, whether in children's soccer leagues or Little League baseball or in professional sports. Although we can all think of bad examples of coaches who were overly competitive, for the most part we think competition in sports is a good system, and we think it fair that the best teams receive some prize or award at the end. (See 1 Corinthians 9:25-26 and 2 Timothy 2:5 for some metaphors of athletic competition that Paul uses in a positive way.)

Similarly, in our school system, the assigning of grades is a competitive activity in which the best math students and the best English students and the best art and music students receive higher grades. The grading system provides guidance to help students find something they can do well. When I fly in an airplane, I am glad that it has been designed by someone who got straight A's in mathematics and engineering! The grading system is "competitive," and *it guides society in assigning jobs* to those who are best suited to those jobs.

In the business world, competition does that as well. We hired a careless painter once for our house, and he lasted only a day. But then we found a good painter, and we were willing to pay more for his high-quality work. The bad painter needed to find another occupation, and we were helping him do that by asking him not to come back the next day. The world is so diverse, and the economic system has so many needs, that I am sure there is some area in which he can fulfill a need and do well. But it wasn't painting.

We must recognize, of course, that in every society there will be some people who because of physical or mental disability are unable to find productive work without help from others, either from charitable organizations or from government agencies. Surely we should support such efforts to provide a "safety net" for those unable to care for themselves. But in American society at least (with which I am most familiar), and in many other countries as well, there is productive work available for the vast majority of the population, and competition is the mechanism that helps workers find the jobs for which their interests and abilities best suit them.

So a competitive system is one in which we test our abilities and find if we can do something better than others, and so be paid for it. The system works well when we reward better work and greater quantity of work with greater reward.

In fact, if you have ever shopped around for the lowest price on a shirt or a computer or a car, your actions show that you approve of competition in the economy, because you are making competition work. You are buying from the person who can produce and distribute a computer cheaper than someone else, and you are encouraging that more efficient manufacturer to stay in business, and you are discouraging the less efficient, more expensive computer manufacturers from staying in business. This happens every day, and we take it for granted. This should cause us to realize that if we are going to be good stewards of our possessions we need to have competition in the marketplace.

Another benefit of competition is that people keep getting better at making things, and as a result the (inflation-adjusted) prices of consumer goods keep falling over the course of decades. This means that over time an economically competitive society will enjoy an increasingly higher standard of living.

The CD player that I bought last week cost me $89, but a year ago it would have cost me $120. Similarly, computers keep getting better and prices keep falling, so more and more people can afford a computer, and everyone who buys one has more money left over than he or she would have had a year ago. The first pocket calculators cost around $100, but today I can buy one at the checkout counter at the drug store for $1. These are examples of how competition brings economic benefit to the society as a whole.

There is still another benefit to competition. God has created us with a desire to do well, and to improve what we are able to do. Competition spurs us on to do better, because we see others doing better and we decide we can do that too. An executive from a company that made mail-sorting machines once told me that his engineers thought they had made the fastest, quietest mail sorting machine possible—until he took them to watch a machine manufactured by a German company that was even faster and even quieter! Then the engineers went back to work, determined to do even better. I think that God has made us with such a desire to strive for excellence in our work so that, in doing this, we would imitate his excellence more fully.

A kind of competition to try to do as well as or better than someone else seems to be what Solomon had in mind when he wrote,

> Then I saw that all toil and all skill in work come from a man's envy of his neighbor (Eccles. 4:4).

The term translated "envy" (in most translations) or "rivalry" (NASB) is the Hebrew word *qin'āh,* a term that can have either negative or positive moral connotations, depending on the context (much like our terms "jealousy" and "zeal"). Here it seems to have the sense "competitive spirit."[1] The verse does not say this is good or bad, only that it happens. (A different word, *chāmad,* is used in Exodus 20:17 when God says, "You shall not covet.") People see what someone else has, and they decide to work harder themselves, or to gain better skills. In this way, competition spurs people on to better work, and they themselves prosper, and society prospers.

There is in fact a sort of mild "competition" implied in the testing of men before they become deacons:

> And let them also be tested first; then let them serve as deacons if they prove themselves blameless (1 Tim. 3:10).

If they do well in the time of testing ("if they prove themselves blameless"), then they can become deacons. If not, then they should find some other area of service within the church.

Competition seems to be the system God intended when he gave people greater talents in one area and gave other people greater talents in another area, and when he established a world where justice and fairness would require giving greater reward for better work.

Competition brings many opportunities to glorify God, as we try to use our talents to their full potential and thus manifest the God-like abilities that he has granted to us, with thankfulness in our hearts to him. Competition enables each person to find a role in which he or she can make a positive contribution to society and thus a role in which people can work in a way that serves others by doing good for them. Competition is thus a sort of societal functioning of God's attributes of wisdom and kindness, and it is a way society helps people discover God's will for their lives. Competition also enables us individually to demonstrate fairness and kindness toward others, even those with whom we compete.

On the other hand, competition brings many temptations to sin. There is a difference between trying to do a job better than others, on the one hand, and trying to harm others and prevent them from earning a living on the other hand. There is nothing wrong with trying to run a better car repair shop than the one down the street, but there is a lot wrong with lying about the other mechanic, or stealing his tools, or in my heart seeking to do him harm.

Competition also brings temptations to pride, and to excessive work that allows no rest or time with family or with God. There is also the temptation to so distort life values that we become unable even to enjoy the fruits of our labor.

But the distortions of something good must not cause us to think that the thing itself is evil. These temptations to sin should not obscure the fact that competition in itself, within appropriate limits (some of which should be established by government), is good and pleasing to God, and provides many opportunities to glorify him.

9

BORROWING AND LENDING

*Borrowing and lending are fundamentally good and
provide many opportunities for glorifying God,
but also many temptations to sin*

SOMETIMES CHRISTIANS HAVE read Old Testament passages
that speak against lending money at interest (what the King
James Version called "usury"), and they have had an uneasy
conscience about borrowing or lending money at interest
because of these passages. But if we look at those passages in
detail, and understand them in their proper historical context,
they seem only to prohibit taking advantage of the poor in their
poverty (see Ex. 22:25; Lev. 25:35-37; Deut. 23:19; Neh. 5:7-
10; Ps. 15:5; Prov. 28:8; Luke 6:34). There are other passages,
even in the Old Testament, that assume that people will borrow
some things (see Ex. 22:14; 2 Kings 4:3), and some verses regulate the process of lending:

> "When you make your neighbor a loan of any sort, you shall
> not go into his house to collect his pledge" (Deut. 24:10).

The phrase, "when you make your neighbor a loan," assumes that the people of Israel would loan things to one another. Therefore it assumes that some of them would borrow from others (for you cannot loan something unless someone else borrows it). Therefore even in the Old Testament there was no absolute prohibition on loans.

In fact, some verses encourage lending and commend the man who lends:

> It is well with the man who deals generously and lends;
>   who conducts his affairs with justice (Ps. 112:5;
> see also Ps. 37:26).

I do not think that Romans 13:8 ("owe no one anything") prohibits all borrowing or even discourages borrowing, for taken in context it simply says we should pay what we owe when we owe it. If we look at the statement in its proper context, translated to show the connection between verse 7 and verse 8 (as is done in the recently published *English Standard Version*), it reads as follows:

> For the same reason you also pay taxes, for the authorities are ministers of God, attending to this very thing. Pay to all *what is owed* to them: taxes to whom taxes are *owed,* revenue to whom revenue is *owed,* respect to whom respect is *owed,* honor to whom honor is *owed. Owe* no one anything, except to love each other, for the one who loves another has fulfilled the law (Rom. 13:6-8).

As is evident in this translation, the command, "owe no one anything," is simply a summary of the obligations to pay what we owe as specified in the previous verses, whether taxes or respect or honor or so forth. Therefore, if I have a mortgage on my house, I should make the mortgage payments when they are "owed"; that is, I should make payments on time as I have agreed to do. I do not "owe" the entire balance of the mortgage to the lender until the date specified. Though I have borrowed money and am carrying a long-term debt, I am completely obedient to Romans 13:8, "owe no one anything," because I have no past-due payments on my mortgage.

Of course, borrowing may at times be unwise (see Prov. 22:7, "the borrower is the slave of the lender"; also Deut. 28:12), and the ability to borrow may be misused by those who incur excessive debt ("The wicked borrows but does not pay back," Ps. 37:21), and borrowing does carry some risk and some obligations that can be very hard to get out of (see Ex. 22:14), but the Bible does not say that borrowing in itself is wrong.

It seems to me, therefore, that borrowing and lending in themselves are not prohibited by God, for many places in the Bible assume that these things will happen.

Jesus even seems to approve lending money at interest, not to the poor who need it to live (as in the Old Testament passages quoted above), but to the bankers who borrow the money from us so that they can use it to make more money:

> "Why then did you not put my money in the bank, and at my coming I might have collected it with interest?" (Luke 19:23; also Matt. 25:27).

When we understand what borrowing really is, we will realize that the process of borrowing and lending is another wonderful gift that God has given to us as human beings. It is another activity that is unique among human beings, for animals don't borrow or lend or pay interest, nor could they even understand the process.

What are borrowing and lending? In itself, lending is the temporary transfer of the control of property but not of the ownership of property. This wonderful process allows the lender to have an infinite variety of choices with respect to the following factors:

(a) Control: I have an infinite variety of choices between keeping an item and giving it away. I can lend you my car and come with you while you run your errand, or I can lend it to you for one brief errand, or I can lend it to you without restrictions for a day or a week or a year.

(b) Amount: I can lend you a small item (such as my pocket knife) or a large item (such as my car or house), and there are all sorts of choices in between.

(c) Risk: there is very small risk in letting my wife borrow my car keys or my jacket, but there is very large risk in letting a total stranger borrow my car, and there are all sorts of choices in between.

Borrowing also allows the borrower an infinite variety of choices between no use of an item and owning the item. I can rent a car for a day, a week, or a month, thus allowing me to have little use, or some use, or much use of the car, without actually owning it.

The great value of borrowing and lending is that they multiply the usefulness of all the wealth of a society. My local library may have only one copy of a reference book, but 300 people might use it in a year, *thus giving my community approximately as much value as 300 copies of that book* if each person had to buy one.

I own a car in Arizona, but because of the process of borrowing and lending, I can fly into any city in the United States and have the use of a rental car for a day, without having to own a car in that city. The existence of the wonderful mechanism of borrowing and lending thus *gives me approximately as much value as owning thousands of cars,* one in each city that I may want to fly to in the whole world! And it does the same for every other person in society. The same is true for hotel rooms, apartments, lake cabins, boats, formal clothing for weddings, trucks and trailers for moving things, and thousands of other goods that can be rented for a time. In this way, the process of borrowing and lending multiplies the available wealth in the world more times than it is possible to calculate.

The same kinds of benefits occur with borrowing and lending money. When I borrow money to buy a house or start a business, I enjoy the usefulness of that money (just as I enjoy the usefulness of a rental car) for a period of time without actually having to own the money myself. Just as I pay a fee for the rental car while I use it, so I pay a "rental fee" for the money while I use it (this rental fee is called interest). Borrowing the money and using it for a time is far easier than obtaining all the money myself before I can gain the use of it.

The process of borrowing and lending money also means that more people can use the money, just as more people can use a rental car. To take a simplified example, let's say a banker has $90,000 sitting in his bank vault doing no good for anybody, just sitting there. But you want to buy a house for $100,000, and you only have $10,000. It would take you many years to save the additional $90,000 to buy that house. But the banker loans you $90,000, and suddenly the money is doing some good—it enables you to buy and live in the house. (And you pay the banker 6 percent "interest" on the use of the money, or $5,400 per year, which makes the banker happy as well.)

The story does not stop there, however. You pay the $100,000 to the builder of the house. Let's say the builder in turn puts $80,000 of that money *back in the very same bank* for a while. The banker now sees that $80,000 sitting in his bank vault, doing nothing worthwhile, so he loans part of it (say $70,000) to Person B, who uses it to buy an $80,000 house.[1] Once again, that home builder puts *the same money back in the very same bank,* let's say $60,000 this time. So then the banker loans out $50,000 of this money to Person C, and by this time the same "useless" money that was sitting in the bank vault has been used three times to enable three separate people to buy houses. And the process goes on and on. Thus, borrowing and lending *multiply the usefulness of money many times over.* (It is a technical task for economists to calculate just how many times it multiplies, given various interest rates and other factors in the economy.)

This process is not just "smoke and mirrors" with no reality behind it. You *really are* making use of the $90,000, and you *really are* living in your own house, just as you *really are* using the rental car when you visit another city. The difference is that you can't both use the rental car and return it to be rented by someone else at the same time, but you *can* do that with money.

What is true of buying a house is also true of starting a business. Very few people have enough money on hand to buy the equipment needed to start a new business. But when people can borrow the money, they can get their businesses running and then pay back the loan from the money they earn. Such loans to start small businesses ("microloans" for "microenterprises") are starting to have an amazing impact among the poor in many countries of the world.[2] Through the amazing process of borrowing and lending, the usefulness of money is multiplied and even very poor people are able to start profitable businesses and work their way out of poverty.

The point is that if we could not borrow and lend money, but had to operate only on a cash basis, the world would have a vastly lower standard of living, not only in the richer nations but also in the poorer nations as well. The existence of borrowing and lending means that the total available amount of goods and services in the world has been multiplied many times over.

In this way, borrowing and lending multiply phenomenally our God-given enjoyment of the material creation, and our potential for being thankful to God for all these things and glorifying him through our use of them.

In borrowing and lending, we can reflect many of God's attributes. We can demonstrate trustworthiness and faithful stewardship, honesty, wisdom, and thanksgiving. We can demonstrate some knowledge of the distant future, and love and mercy and thankfulness to God.

However, there are temptations to sin that accompany borrowing. As many Americans are now discovering, there is a great temptation to borrow more than is wise, or to borrow for things they can't afford and don't need, and thus they become foolishly entangled in interest payments that reflect poor stewardship and wastefulness, and that entrap people in a downward spiral of more and more debt. In addition, lenders can be greedy or selfish. Some lenders will lend to people who have no reasonable expectation of repaying and then take advantage of these people in their poverty and distress.

Christians who work in the business world tell me that one of their greatest frustrations is "collections": Customers owe money and they won't pay their bills! Christians who take the Bible as God's Word have to realize that God tells us to pay our bills when they are due: "Owe no one anything" (Rom. 13:8) surely means we should pay our bills on time! People who fail to pay bills when they are due are not viewed positively in Scripture, for it says, "The wicked borrows but does not pay back" (Ps. 37:21). Failing to pay a bill when we have said we would is also failing to keep our word, and it dishonors our Creator, who always keeps his word.

But the distortions of something good must not cause us to think that the thing itself is evil. Borrowing and lending are wonderful, uniquely human abilities that are good in themselves and pleasing to God and bring many opportunities for glorifying him. Because borrowing and lending are such good things, I expect that there will be borrowing and lending even in heaven, not to overcome poverty but to multiply our abilities to glorify and enjoy God. (But I don't know what the interest rate will be!)

10

ATTITUDES OF HEART

THE TEN COMMANDMENTS end with a reminder that God is concerned not only with our actions but also with our attitudes of heart, for God says,

> "You shall not covet . . . anything that is your neighbor's" (Ex. 20:17).

Although I have touched on this concern at various points, it is appropriate that we end our analysis of these aspects of business by remembering that in every aspect of business activity, God knows our hearts, and we must glorify him by having attitudes of heart in which he delights.

> Let the words of my mouth *and the meditation of my heart*
>   be acceptable in your sight,
>   O LORD, my rock and my redeemer (Ps. 19:14).

> He knows the secrets of the heart (Ps. 44:21; see also Luke 16:15; Acts 15:8).

Therefore in all our ownership of property, and in all our stewardship, if we want to glorify God in business, we should seek to avoid pride and to have hearts full of love and humility toward others and toward God. In producing goods and services for others, and in using them for our own enjoyment, we should have hearts of thanksgiving to God for his goodness in providing these things to us. If we work for someone else, we should work as if we were working

> for the Lord and not for men, knowing that from the Lord
> you will receive the inheritance as your reward (Col. 3:23-24).

And if others work for us, we need to think of them as equal in value as human beings made in the image of God, and our heart's desire should be that the job bring them good and not harm. We should be thankful to God for money and profit, but we should never *love* money or profit. We are to love God and our neighbor instead.

And so all business activity tests our hearts. The good things that God gives us through business are very good, but we must always remember that God is infinitely better! David said, "If riches increase, set not your heart on them" (Ps. 62:10), and another psalmist said, "Whom have I in heaven but you? And there is nothing on earth that I desire besides you" (Ps. 73:25). Are our hearts set on God above all, or on the things that God gives? Jesus said, "You shall love the Lord your God with all your heart . . ." (Matt. 22:37), and "You cannot serve God and money" (Matt. 6:24).

If we love God above all, as we look at all of the business activities in the world around us, we will see evil mixed with good, and then our hearts should feel sorrow and grief when we see God's commands being disobeyed and his purposes violated. But our hearts should also be filled with joy and thanksgiving and praise to him for the wonders of his creation, and for his remarkable wisdom in designing so many amazing ways in which business activity in itself is fundamentally good and brings glory to God.

11

EFFECT ON WORLD POVERTY

UP TO THIS POINT I have been encouraging you, as a reader, to change your attitudes to many of the components of business activity. I do not want you to feel vaguely guilty about business, and I do not want you even to feel simply that business is morally neutral but does some good because at least it is a means of advancing the gospel. Of course I agree that business is a wonderful means of advancing the gospel, and I rejoice in it and thank God that thousands of businesses around the world do much personally and financially to advance the gospel.

But I have been aiming at something more. I want you not to feel vague guilt about business activities but rather to *rejoice* in the God-given *goodness of business in itself* pursued in obedience to God. I want you, as a reader, to *enjoy* and thank God for:

1. Ownership
2. Productivity
3. Employment

4. Commercial transactions

5. Profit

6. Money

7. Inequality of possessions

8. Competition, and

9. Borrowing and lending.

At this point, however, some will think, what about the poor? What about those who own almost nothing, who cannot buy and sell, cannot make a profit, have no money, and have no opportunity to compete? What good does all of this do for them?

As I said in chapter 7 above, we should always to seek to help the poor and seek to overcome their poverty. John says, "If anyone has the world's goods and sees his brother in need, yet closes his heart against him, how does God's love abide in him?" (1 John 3:17). And Paul says in Galatians 2:10, "they asked us to remember the poor, the very thing I was eager to do" (Gal. 2:10; see also Matt. 25:39-40; Acts 2:45; 4:35; Rom. 12:13; 15:25-27; Eph. 4:28; Titus 3:14; Heb. 13:16).

But *how* should we remember the poor? *How* should we open our hearts to our brother in need? A short-term solution is to give food and clothing to the poor, and that is certainly right. But it is no long-term solution, for the food is soon eaten and the clothing wears out.

I believe *the only long-term solution to world poverty is business.* That is because businesses produce goods, and businesses produce jobs. And businesses continue producing goods year after year, and continue providing jobs and paying wages year after year. Therefore if we are ever going to see *long-term* solutions to world poverty, I believe it will come through starting and maintaining productive, profitable businesses.

In large measure this will come about through starting businesses in poor countries and in poor neighborhoods in developed countries. Another, less visible way businesses help overcome poverty is through increasing efficiency and productivity, and thus making quality goods less expensive, in the world market. Because competitive, profitable businesses in developed countries have caused the price of a solar-powered pocket calculator to drop from $100 to $1, even a businessman with a $237 microloan can afford a calculator for his new business.

But if that is true, if the solution to world poverty is business rightly pursued, then why hasn't business solved world poverty already? One reason is that there are too many obstacles.

As I mentioned above, in many poor countries excessive government red tape effectively prevents entrepreneurs from legally owning property or businesses, and economic growth is stopped before it can begin.[1] Another, sometimes related obstacle is a sinful misuse of business power to benefit only a tiny number of people and to prevent others from starting competing businesses. Another obstacle is evil governments that confiscate a country's wealth and thus prevent businesses from helping people overcome poverty. Yet another is repressive governments that hinder and destroy businesses in order to enhance their own power.[2] Another obstacle preventing businesses from solving the problem of poverty is weak governments that do not punish crime or fraud,[3] and do not enforce contracts or establish a sound banking and court system. These are major problems that can only be overcome when those who hold the power in such poorer countries resolve to love their neighbor as themselves and put the good of the country ahead of retaining power and privilege for themselves and their friends.[4]

But I think another large reason business activity has not yet solved world poverty is *negative attitudes toward business in the world community.* And these negative attitudes also lead to and aggravate those other problems that I just mentioned.

If people think business is evil, they will hesitate to start businesses, and they will never feel real freedom to enjoy working in business, because it will always be tainted with the faint cloud of false guilt. Who can enjoy being an *evil* materialist who works with *evil* money to earn *evil* profits by *exploiting* laborers and producing material goods that feed people's *evil* greed and enhance their *evil* pride and sustain their *evil* inequality of possessions and feed their *evil* competitiveness? Who wants to devote his life to such an evil pursuit as business? What government would ever want to establish laws and policies that would encourage such an evil thing as business? If business is evil, then why not tax it and regulate it until it can barely survive? And so with the attitude that business is fundamentally evil in all its parts, business activity is hindered at every point, and poverty remains. (In fact, if the devil himself wanted to keep people created by God in the wretched bondage of lifelong poverty, it is hard to think of a better way he could do it than to make people think that business is fundamentally evil, so they would avoid entering into it or would oppose it at every turn. And so I suspect that a profoundly negative attitude toward business in itself—not toward distortions and abuses, but toward business activity in itself—is ultimately a lie of the Enemy who wants to keep God's people from fulfilling his purposes.)

But what if Christians could change their attitudes toward business, and what if Christians could begin to change the attitudes of the world toward business?

If attitudes toward business change in the ways I have described, then who could resist being a *God-pleasing* subduer of the earth who uses materials from God's *good* creation and works with the *God-given* gift of money to earn morally *good* profits, and shows *love* to his neighbors by giving them jobs and by producing material *goods* that overcome world poverty, goods that enable people to *glorify God* for his goodness, that sustain *just* and *fair* differences in possessions, and that encourage morally *good* and *beneficial* competition? What a great career that would be! What a great activity for governments to favor and encourage! What a solution to world poverty! What a great way to give glory to God!

NOTES

PREFACE

1. The paper has been published in its original form in *On Kingdom Business: Transforming Missions Through Entrepreneurial Strategies,* edited by Tetsunao Yamamori and Kenneth A. Eldred (Wheaton, Ill.: Crossway, 2003), 127-151. The book contains a remarkable collection of case studies from Christians who are running successful businesses in what many would think the most unlikely countries in the world today.

INTRODUCTION

1. All emphases in Scripture quotations were added by the author.

CHAPTER 1: OWNERSHIP

1. See Hernando de Soto, *The Mystery of Capital: Why Capitalism Triumphs in the West and Fails Everywhere Else* (New York: Basic Books, 2000). The research team headed by de Soto tried opening a small garment workshop (with one worker) on the outskirts of Lima, Peru. They worked at the registration process six hours a day and it took them 289 days! The cost was $1,231, or thirty-one times the monthly minimum wage (approximately three years' salary). They add, "To obtain legal authorization to build a house on state-owned land took six years and eleven months requiring 207 administrative steps in fifty-two government offices. . . . To obtain a legal title for that piece of land took 728 steps" (19-20). They detail similar labyrinthine bureaucratic roadblocks to property ownership in other countries such as Egypt, the Philippines, and Haiti, and conclude that legal ownership of property or even a small business is effectively impossible for the vast majority of the population in many Third World countries.

CHAPTER 6: MONEY

1. Wayne Grudem, *Systematic Theology: An Introduction to Biblical Doctrine* (Leicester, U.K.: InterVarsity, and Grand Rapids, Mich.: Zondervan, 1994).

2. *The American Heritage Dictionary of the English Language* (Boston: Houghton Mifflin, 1992), 1166.

CHAPTER 7: INEQUALITY OF POSSESSIONS

1. See especially 1 Cor. 3:12-15; also Dan. 12:2; Matt. 6:10, 20-21; 19:21; Luke 6:22-23; 12:18-21, 32, 42-48; 14:13-14; 1 Cor. 3:8; 9:18; 13:3; 15:19, 29-32, 58; Gal. 6:9-10; Eph. 6:7-8; Phil. 4:17; Col. 3:23-24; 1 Tim. 6:18; Heb. 10:34, 35; 11:10, 14-16, 26, 35; 1 Pet. 1:4; 2 John 8; Rev. 11:18; 22:12; see also Matt. 5:46; 6:2-6, 16-18, 24; Luke 6:35.

CHAPTER 8: COMPETITION

1. The definition "competitive spirit" is given for this word in this verse by Koehler-Baumgartner, *Hebrew and Aramaic Lexicon of the Old Testament,* 1110.

CHAPTER 9: BORROWING AND LENDING

1. Banks of course cannot loan out all of their money or they would fail; so governments set reserve requirements for the proportion that can be loaned out again. Actual reserve requirements are not taken into account in this simplified example, but the general principle of loaning much of the money out again still applies.

2. An excellent example of the use of such microloans (often $500 or less) to start small businesses in poor areas of the world is seen in the pioneering work of Opportunity International in Oak Brook, Illinois. In 2002 they made 536,033 loans, and the average loan amount was $237. Their annual report shows loan recipients with profitable businesses such as flower stalls, sugar stalls, bakeries, manufacturing of dyed cloth, pottery, or baskets, and raising chickens or fish. Money is loaned at market rates, and the loan repayment rate

is 98 percent! They estimate these loans are providing 800,000 jobs and impacting the lives of 4,000,000 people. (See the editorial on Opportunity International, "Compassionate Capitalism," by Jack Kemp and Christopher Crane, *Washington Times,* Aug. 27, 2003; www.washingtontimes.com.)

CHAPTER 11: EFFECT ON WORLD POVERTY

1. See the reference in chapter 1, note 1 to Hernando de Soto, *The Mystery of Capital.*

2. For example, a *Wall Street Journal* editorial pointed out an increasingly hostile environment for businesses in modern-day Russia: "Security forces are interfering in business activities when and where they choose. The attorney general's office rubber stamps accusations against oligarchs and big businesses upon orders from the Kremlin, while local prosecutors are on a business-bashing quest to meet the expectations of their governors and mayors" ("KGB State," by Gary Kasparov, *Wall Street Journal,* Sept. 18, 2003, A16).

3. This problem is also found in modern Russia, for example, from which we hear frequent reports of widespread Mafia control of large segments of the economy.

4. There are a number of studies that outline the legal and societal factors necessary to allow for sustained economic growth to occur in a country. See, for example, Brian Griffiths, *The Creation of Wealth* (London: Hodder and Stoughton, 1984; Downers Grove Ill.: InterVarsity, 1985).

GENERAL INDEX

SCRIPTURE INDEX